Knights and castles /
940.1 DAR

7978

Dargie, Richard.
KENDALL ELEMENTARY SCHOOL

W9-DGY-047

7978

940.1
DAR   Dargie, Richard

         Knights and cas-
         tles

DUE DATE	BRODART	02/99	25.69

The Age of Castles
KNIGHTS AND CASTLES

Richard Dargie

RSVP
RAINTREE
STECK-VAUGHN
PUBLISHERS
A Steck-Vaughn Company

Austin, Texas

Kendall Elementary School
Library Media Center
2408 Meadow Lakes Drive
Naperville, IL 60564

The Age of Castles

Titles in this series
CASTLE LIFE
CASTLE UNDER SIEGE
HOW CASTLES WERE BUILT
KNIGHTS AND CASTLES

© Copyright 1999, text, Steck-Vaughn Company

All rights reserved. No part of this book may be reproduced or utilized in any
form or by any means, electronic or mechanical, including photocopying, recording, or by any
information storage and retrieval system, without permission in writing from the Publisher.
Inquiries should be addressed to: Copyright Permissions,
Steck-Vaughn Company, P.O. Box 26015, Austin, TX 78755.

Published by Raintree Steck-Vaughn Publishers,
an imprint of Steck-Vaughn Company

Library of Congress Cataloging-in-Publication Data
Dargie, Richard.
Knights and castles / Richard Dargie.
p.   cm.—(Age of castles)
Includes bibliographical references and index.
Summary: Traces the history of knights from the early middle ages through
the end of the fifteenth century, with information on their training, duties,
the castles they lived in, and their role in medieval society.
ISBN 0-8172-5122-7 (hard); 0-8172-8122-3 (soft)
1. Knights and Knighthood—Juvenile literature.
2. Castles—Juvenile literature.
3. Civilization, Medieval—Juvenile literature.
[1. Knights and knighthood. 2. Castles. 3. Civilization, Medieval.]
I. Title. II. Series.
CR4513.D37 1999
940.1'088'355—dc21   98-7003

Printed in Italy. Bound in the United States.
1 2 3 4 5 6 7 8 9 0 03 02 01 00 99

Cover pictures: Muiderslot Castle, Holland; a Knight Templar; shields with coats of arms.

PICTURE ACKNOWLEDGMENTS
The publishers wish to thank the following for permission to publish their pictures: (t=top; c=center;
b=bottom; l=left; r=right) AKG London 9b, 27r, 29t, 36, 37; Bridgeman Art Library, London/New
York, /Bibliothèque Nationale, Paris 7t, 21t, 22, 30, 31t, /Bargello, Florence 7bl, /British Library,
London 9t, 17r, 41t, /Pinacoteca di Brera, Milan 17l, /British Museum, London 31b, /Private Collection
41b; British Library, London 7r, 11t, 14; British Museum 12, 23bl, 23br, 28, 29b, 38; © Bodleian
Library, University of Oxford, 1998, *MS.Bodley 264, part 1, 12, 102*, 24; Dean and Chapter, Durham
University 15tl; E.T. Archive 5, 8, 15r, 34, 42; Image Bank 18; Robert Harding 6; Stockmarket 23t; The
Board and Trustees of the Armouries *IX.915, IX,1081, 25, IV.411*, 33; The Master and Fellows of
Corpus Christi College, Cambridge 19b; Topham 35, 43; Wayland Picture Library 16; Werner Forman
Archive 39. Illustrator: Peter Dennis. Project artwork: John Yates

CONTENTS

⊠ ⊠ ⊠ ⊠

THE FIRST KNIGHTS

WARRIORS ON HORSEBACK

"**G**ET THE HORSES ON THE BEACH!" The Duke stands at the prow of his ship and roars instructions to his men. They carry their weapons and armor to the shore. The Normans must build a camp by nightfall, before the enemy arrives. If they win the battle tomorrow, the men will be made knights, given land, and allowed to build castles.

Norman knights invaded much of
Europe in the years after A.D. 1050. They
controlled part of France, England, and
Sicily. The Normans were difficult to defeat in battle.
They were protected by coats of chain mail, long shields,
and helmets of iron. Their knights were excellent horsemen.
They used stirrups to keep themselves steady in the saddle when fighting
with their favorite weapon, the lance.

The Normans were not the first knights. In the years after A.D. 800, the great Christian emperor Charlemagne had trained an army to fight on horseback. His knights needed to travel quickly. They had to defend the distant points of his European kingdom against Vikings from Scandinavia and against Arabs from North Africa. Charlemagne's soldiers were the first knights of medieval Europe.

◁ Like the Vikings, the Normans used ships to move their knights and supplies quickly.

KNIGHT SUPPLIES

In A.D. 806, Charlemagne called together his knights (above) with these instructions:

"Each knight must bring a shield, lance, sword, dagger, bow, and quiver. Bring carts with spades, axes, picks, iron-pointed stakes, and all other things needed for war. Take enough food and clothing for six months."

A KNIGHT AND HIS CASTLE

Stonemasons have completed work on the knight's castle. Strong and safe, it shows off his great wealth. While he admires his new home, the knight remembers the vows he has made to his king. He has promised to uphold the king's law and to protect the land. Tomorrow, he will listen to the complaints of his peasants.

△ Chepstow Castle was begun before 1070 to keep the Welsh from attacking English towns along the Severn River valley.

Castles were built to defend towns and villages across medieval Europe. It was the knight's duty to defend his castle and keep it in good condition. The king's most trusted knights were given castles near enemy lands. Chepstow Castle, shown above, guarded the border between Wales and England.

◁ A French knight supervises wine making in his castle yard. Wine was stored for use in sieges.

A knight could live well on the produce of his castle estate. One noble complained: "These knights of ours are laden not with steel but with wine, not with spears but with cheeses, not with swords but with roasting spits. You would think they were on their way to feast, and not to fight."

CHIVALRY

Knights, like Sir Geoffrey Luttrell shown above, lived by a set of rules called chivalry. They promised to use their strength to perform good deeds, defend women, and protect the weak.

The knight went everywhere on horseback. He depended on his riding skills for survival in battle. He practiced them by hunting foxes and deer in the forests. The castle's horses were cared for by the marshal and his grooms.

▷ A knight from a medieval chess set. Chess was a popular game in the castle.

LEARNING TO BE A KNIGHT

HOW TO BEHAVE

"**M**ORE DRINK HERE, BOY!" shouts the knight. A page scuttles to the kitchen to search for a fresh jug of wine. Other pages carry platters of freshly roasted swan to the table. The minstrels take up their pipes and play a new song from France.

At about the age of seven, the son of a knight or noble was often sent to a neighboring castle to serve as a page. The page learned to read and to serve his lord and was taught the skills needed to run a castle and the farms on its estate. At fourteen, he could become a "squire," the personal attendant of a knight.

△ Pages serving at a banquet for French knights who belonged to a brotherhood called the Order of the Star

Squires had to dress their knights properly for battle and for hunting. They had to keep the knight's weapons and armor clean and ready for use. Squires also learned good manners and the laws of chivalry. Knowing how to behave properly could help a poor squire find a rich wife with lands and a castle.

▷ Squires dress their knight so that he will impress the ladies of the castle.

A PEACEFUL WEEKEND

Knights in a strong castle, like this one at Muiderslot in Holland, became very powerful. Church leaders were afraid that they would use their power to attack merchants and peasants. Many churches passed laws forcing knights to follow their vows of chivalry. The earliest, passed in 1041, was called the Truce of God. It outlawed any fighting on Fridays, Saturdays, and Sundays.

HOW TO FIGHT

The scarred old sergeant barks out commands, and the boys set to work eagerly. Some practice fighting at close quarters, swinging clubs against their opponents' shields. A page learning to joust is pulled along on a wooden horse by two friends. A mounted squire tilts at a mechanical device called a quintain. The castle yard resounds as metal, wood, and leather clash.

Medieval swords were long and made of steel, and they were very heavy. It took great strength to wield them in battle. Young pages built up their sword arms by training with special clubs made of wood and lead. Squires learned to use heavy lances by jousting at the quintain. When they struck this target, a weighted bag swung around to unhorse any careless riders.

△ Young squires are toughened up for battle with exercises that test their bravery and endurance.

▷ Local peasants are trained in archery so that they can help defend the castle.

The castellan was in charge of the castle soldiers. It was his job to make sure that every man could help in wartime. The local serfs had no horses, so they were trained as foot soldiers. Every Sunday, the castellan made them practice hard with spears and bows.

Kendall Elementary School
Library Media Center
2408 Meadow Lakes Drive
Naperville, IL 60564

THE RULES OF WAR

A squire watches his master ride out to meet an enemy knight in single combat. The faces of both knights are hidden behind great helms, but the squire can recognize the special "coat of arms" that decorates his master's horse and armor. After many heavy blows, the enemy knight falls exhausted. The winning knight commands his squire: "Take this prisoner to my tent, and bind up his wounds."

Knights could win honor by challenging a rival to single combat. They preferred to fight other knights, for there was nothing chivalrous about defeating a commoner. If a knight captured an opponent, he could demand a ransom from his prisoner. This ransom was paid with valuables or through the performance of a special task.

△ In France, Germany, and England, drawings like these recorded the coats of arms of every knight.

DESIGN A COAT OF ARMS

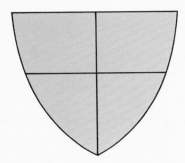

Brave and true

1. Cut a piece of cardboard into the shape of a shield. Draw lines dividing it into four.

2. Draw an object in each of the areas. Choose objects that show your name, interests, hobbies, or star sign.

3. Curl the ends of a strip of paper by wrapping them around a pencil. Write a motto on the paper and fasten it to your shield.

Every knight displayed his own special coat of arms on his tunic, shield, and horse. This meant that he could identify friends and enemies in battle. The Italian knight Guido da Fogliano dressed all his men in uniforms bearing his symbol of black diamonds. Officials called heralds kept lists of the colors and coats of arms of every knight in Europe.

◁ A herald, who watched battles to record the deeds of the brave and the names of the dead

BECOMING A KNIGHT

Trumpets blast, and the herald gives the signal. The knights pull down their helmet visors and begin to charge. Lances level, they take aim. The crowd cheers as the wooden lances smash and splinter into a thousand pieces. One knight falls from his horse. Watching from the castle battlements, his lady swoons with fright.

After 1400, it was possible to buy knighthoods in many European countries. Consequently, many knights were simply the sons of rich landowners. However, some knights were commoners, dubbed as a reward for heroism in battle. In times of peace, young squires could win knighthoods in jousting tournaments and mock battles.

△ Squires wait with spare lances as two knights in beautifully decorated helmets meet in a joust.

THE OATH

"I vow to serve my liege lord in time of war and to bring forty men to his aid. In time of peace, I vow to keep his laws and to uphold Holy Mother Church."

A knight's oath

▽ The new knight could decorate his shield with his coat of arms.

▷ The fastening of a knight's sword belt was called "girding."

Before he was knighted, a squire had to purify his body. He was bathed and dressed in a white gown. The squire then performed a "vigil." He stayed awake all night, praying at the shrine of a saint and keeping watch over the weapons and armor he would use as a knight.

The squire was now "girded" with his sword. Golden spurs were fastened about his ankles. Then he knelt before his lord, who "dubbed" him by touching a sword to his shoulders. The knight was told: "Let your sword be the defense of widows, orphans, the Church, and all of God's servants."

ON CRUSADE

THE CALL TO ARMS

THE FINEST KNIGHTS from Germany, Italy, and France stand waiting to embark on a crusade. Their ships are fitted out and ready to sail for the Holy Land. Sailors rush up and down the gangplanks, checking that all the supplies and weapons are aboard. The captain looks to the clouds and prays for a fair wind.

△ Crusader ships taking on supplies at Naples in Italy before sailing for Palestine

In the years after 1090, Christian armies set out to many distant lands to fight crusades. These were holy wars fought against warriors with different religious beliefs. Many knights sailed east for Palestine, where Muslims had captured Jerusalem. The crusaders believed that the Muslims had attacked Christian shrines and pilgrims.

◁ An Italian knight receives a blessing before his crusade.

Going on crusade was an act of great chivalry. Some knights dreamed of finding holy relics such as the True Cross on which Christ was crucified. Others hoped to win fame in battle and enter Heaven by dying on crusade. Some simply wanted to gain lands and riches.

A WILD-GOOSE CHASE

Pope Urban II encouraged knights to make the First Crusade in 1095. He preached a fiery sermon to knights gathered in a field near Clermont in France: "Arm yourselves and rescue Jerusalem. Wear Christ's Cross as your badge. If you die in this cause your sins will be pardoned and your soul will go straight to Heaven."

Before the knights of the First Crusade arrived in Jerusalem, a preacher called Peter the Hermit (above) led thousands of peasants to the Holy Land. This was called the People's Crusade. Some of them followed behind a goose that they said contained the Holy Spirit! When Peter's followers landed in Asia, they were massacred by Turks.

HOLDING THE HOLY LAND

The crusader walks along the castle battlements and scans the landscape with his sun-drenched eyes. He can see for miles across the desert. This castle will never be taken by the Muslims. It has the deepest moat in the Christian world. It was built to show the "infidel" that they have lost this land to the Christians forever.

In the Holy Land to the east, and Spain to the west, the crusader knights captured many castles and cities from the Muslims. The Frankish crusader Godfrey de Bouillon became ruler of Jerusalem in 1099. In central Spain, Christian knights built so many castles that the region became known as Castile.

△ Coca Castle in Spain was built of toughened bricks that made it difficult to attack.

▷ A crusader belonging to the feared brotherhood called the Knights Templar

Christian knights had to be rugged to survive in the Holy Land. Water was scarce in the scorching desert, and the Muslims were a fierce enemy. Knights did not always act chivalrously. The crusaders slaughtered thousands of Muslim men, women, and children when they captured Jerusalem in 1099. A Christian priest wrote: "Our men rode in blood up to their knees."

HOLY KNIGHTS

A brotherhood of dedicated warriors called the Knights Templar were much feared by the Muslims. Saladin, the Muslim leader, ordered that all captured Templars should be beheaded. The two shown here are sharing a horse because of their vows of poverty. A priest wrote of the Templars: "I don't know whether to call them monks or knights—they have the meekness of monks but the courage of knights in battle."

A NEW WAY OF LIFE

The gates of the palace courtyard open wide, and the emir welcomes his Frankish friends. He is glad to see them, for they have important business to discuss. Then perhaps they will sip a cool drink while they play chess. The palace musician sings of the new orange harvest, while the slave girls prepare to dance for their Christian visitor.

The crusaders learned a lot from their new Muslim neighbors. The Muslims had libraries and colleges at Cordoba, Damascus, and Baghdad. They were skilled in mathematics, astronomy, medicine, and building castles. Many Arabic words and customs and games, such as chess, were taken back to Europe at this time. Because of the crusades, we still use Arabic numerals today.

Some leaders of the crusades were impressed by their Muslim enemies. The English king Richard the Lionheart praised the wisdom and chivalry of Saladin. Frederick II, the German emperor, learned Arabic so that he could find out more about the Muslims' way of life and their Islamic religion.

THE CHILDREN'S CRUSADE

In 1212, a boy named Nicholas of Cologne had a vision of Jerusalem. Thousands of French and German children then followed him on crusade. Many starved crossing the Alps. Most of the others ended up in the slave markets of North Africa (above).

◁ A Frankish knight meeting a Muslim prince in his busy palace courtyard

THE KNIGHT AT WAR

IN BATTLE

"GOD WITH US!" shout the knights of both armies, but their cries are drowned by the clash of steel. Deadly arrows sing through the air. Wounded horses bray in terror and men scream as they are trampled beneath the knights' steeds.

Blind King John of Bohemia gave a fine example of chivalry at the Battle of Crecy, shown above, in 1346. Although he could not see, he asked to be tied to his horse. Linked to four companions, he charged into the fray and perished.

△ While the archers fight, chivalrous knights stop to watch a duel in the distance.

◁ Built on the border, Alnwick Castle was the scene of many bloody battles between Scottish and English knights.

▽ Unhorsed knights become involved in a bloody mêlée

Knights were not disciplined soldiers. The Italian statesman, Niccolò Machiavelli, said that armies were better off with common foot soldiers. He complained that knights were too interested in chivalry to carry out orders. In the middle of battle, they would seek out rivals and challenge them to a private duel.

A KNIGHT'S TALE

"The mighty maces swing and bones are bashed,
And one knight from his hard-pressed horse has crashed.
The strong war horses stumble; down goes all,
The men are trampled on just like a ball."

Geoffrey Chaucer, *The Canterbury Tales, 1390s*

Medieval battles were murderous events in which soldiers received terrible wounds. As well as swords and lances, knights used pointed daggers that they could thrust through an enemy's visor, bludgeoning maces and hammers that could crush armor and splinter bones, and razor-sharp axes that were said to cut clean through a horse and rider with one blow.

SWORD AND LANCE

It is high summer, the season for battles. A long line of carts makes its way along the dusty track. Some carry weapons and supplies. In others, the wounded suffer in agony. It has been a long campaign. The army needs water and food for the horses. They must reach a friendly castle by nightfall.

△ Knights needed a train of followers to carry armor, weapons, and supplies.

Most knights spent the winter in their castles, feasting, hunting, and preparing for war. In spring, once the muddy roads began to dry, they raised their standards and set off to join the army of their lord. They took the castle blacksmith and armorer with them to keep their swords and lances sharp. The castellan stayed behind with a few guards to protect the knight's family.

◁ The knight's lance, made of ash with a steel tip, is carried by his squire.

MAKING A SWORD HILT

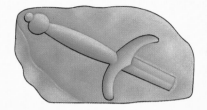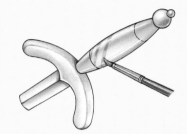

1. Hollow out the shape of a sword hilt in a small block of Plasticine.

2. Mix powdered modeling clay into a liquid and pour in. Leave to dry.

3. Remove the Plasticine. Paint the hilt silver with gold decorations.

Early knights fought with broad, sharp-edged swords that could slash through an enemy's limbs. Many later knights used pointed swords and daggers, which they thrust into gaps in their opponent's plate armor. Sir William Wallace, the Guardian of Scotland, used a sword more than five feet (1.5 m) long. It was so heavy that even a trained knight had to use both hands to wield it.

◁ Swords around 1100 (left) were used to slash through chain mail. Those made after 1400 (far left) were used two-handed to thrust into plate armor.

COATS OF STEEL

In camp, two knights discuss tactics while squires dress them in their armor. First they put on a padded leather "doublet." The squires hang lengths of mail from laces on this doublet and strap on hinged, steel plates, until the knights are completely encased in metal. One knight has put on his padded cap and chain headdress, and a page offers him his magnificent, crested helm.

After 1300, armor was made from steel plates that were hinged and buckled together. Under the plates, most knights wore a coat of iron rings or "chain mail." Metal shoes called sabatons protected his feet. Gauntlets made of intricate steel plates covered his hands. His wrists were defended by hinged, steel plates called cuffs. We still use the word today.

Plate armor suits weighed about 55 lbs. (25kg). They were reasonably comfortable, but very hot. The separate plates allowed the knight enough movement to ride, fight, and even to do headstands. A laced flap in his stockings, or "hose," allowed him to go to the toilet fully armored.

PLATE FOR A POT

◁ Squires dress their knights for battle. The knight on the right displays his coat of arms on his helmet, shield, and tabard.

Not all knights were young. This armor was made for Ulrich IV, governor of Matsch in Germany, when he was elderly. The armor has a special front plate to protect his sagging potbelly. The hinged helmet allowed Ulrich to lift his visor and breathe easily when not fighting.

WAR HORSES

The knight teaches his charger how to kick its front hooves and jump. His warhorse must be able to trample down foes and ride over the dead lying on the ground. The knight wears full armor, so that his mount can learn to carry his full weight in battle.

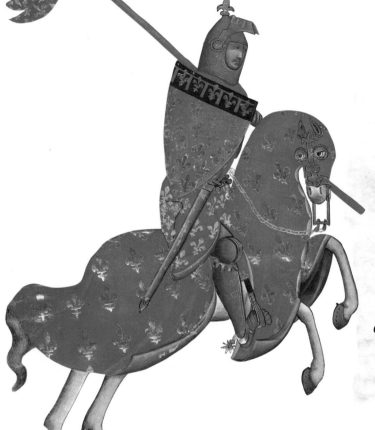

△ This knight displays a dazzling coat of arms on his horse's "caparison."

BLOOD STOCK

A warhorse had many uses in wartime. One Frankish knight wrote in his chronicle:

"In the hot Syrian desert, the Crusaders from France were so thirsty that they took daggers and nicked their horses' veins and drank the blood."

Special warhorses called chargers were bred to carry the armored knight into battle. They were large, powerful animals, with plenty of stamina. A good charger was very expensive and was the knight's most valuable possession. Medieval armies often had to forage over a great distance to find feed for their horses.

◁ Special plate armor was made in the fifteenth century to protect valuable horses from injury in battle.

Knights had several warhorses. It was the squire's duty to hold his master's spare chargers ready during the fighting. He had to provide a fresh horse when his knight's mount was injured or exhausted. According to tradition, Richard III lost the Battle of Bosworth in 1485 because he could not replace his horse and show himself to his men.

BLINKERS AND EARPLUGS

A knight had to protect his horse as well as himself in battle. This manuscript picture shows the "shaffron," which protected the horse's face, and the hinged plates of the "crinet," which guarded the neck. A horse's ears were sometimes plugged with cloth and wax to prevent the horse from being scared by the terrible noise of battle.

AT THE TOURNAMENT

THE MÊLÉE

ONE HUNDRED KNIGHTS enter the paddock and the mêlée begins. Each knight finds a rival to beat down into the dust. One by one the wounded are dragged out until only the champion remains, standing on his bloody sword. His lady salutes him from the stands.

Tournaments were an opportunity for knights to show off their skills in combat. Rich knights displayed their new horses and armor. Poor knights hoped to win a tournament prize. In 1281, a Spanish knight became champion of a tournament held in the kingdom of Aragon. His prize was twenty serfs, five white horses, and a castle.

△ The mêlée was a colorful but terribly dangerous mock battle, which attracted great crowds of spectators.

Tournaments were run according to the laws of chivalry. There were rules about the weapons you could use and about how to behave toward defeated opponents. Heralds made sure that these laws were obeyed. The champion Sir William Marshall, who won more than fifty bloody tournaments, was considered an honorable, chivalrous knight.

◁ A jousting shield shows a knight vowing to defend his lady.

△ Heralds point out the colors of competing knights.

A KNIGHTLY POEM

*"Jousts were called, ladies to see
Great lords came there a-plenty.
Tournaments attired in the field,
A thousand knights with spear and shield,
Knights began together to ride,
Some were unhorsed on every side."*

Iponydon, a medieval poem

Tournaments were held in peacetime so that knights could practice for war. Sometimes knights fought to the death to avenge an insult. In one tournament at Cologne in 1240, sixty contestants were killed. After the Pope complained of the death of so many knights, tournaments introduced the use of special blunted weapons.

THE JOUST

Two knights armed with lances thunder down the jousting course. They are allowed three passes, each knight aiming to strike his opponent's chest. Their lances are tipped with wooden tips, or "coronels," which wound but do not kill. Heralds watch to ensure that the laws of chivalry are upheld.

Jousting with lances was a popular tournament event. The aim in most jousts was to break your lance on your opponent's chest rather than to kill him. Some jousters wore armor with panels that sprang off to show a direct hit. After three Frenchmen died in jousting accidents in 1187, King Philip II ordered his knights to use safer lances, tipped with wooden coronels.

A FROG-MOUTHED HELM

This is a "frog-mouthed" jousting helm. It was strapped to a knight's breastplate front and back, so that it could not be torn off by a lance. The knight could see through the eye-slit only when his head was tipped forward, ready for the joust.

◁ In later jousts, the knights charged either side of a barrier, or "tilt," to keep their horses from colliding. Knights wore special armor to protect the chest and jousting arm.

KNIGHTS OF LEGEND

KNIGHTS OF THE ROUND TABLE

A T A FEAST TO CELEBRATE the tournament, a minstrel sings about King Arthur's castle at Camelot. His song tells of the quest to find the Holy Grail, the cup Christ drank from at the Last Supper. His audience gasps as the minstrel describes Arthur's knights seated at the Round Table, imagining they can see the sacred Grail.

Songs about King Arthur were very popular in the Middle Ages. They told how Arthur pulled the magic sword Excalibur from a stone and became a great king. He was so chivalrous that many brave knights came to fight for him and win a place at his Round Table. All went well until Arthur's queen, Guinevere, fell in love with his champion knight, Lancelot.

△ Arthur's knights sat at a round table, so that no knight could claim he was more important than his fellow knights.

◁ **Some people believe that Tintagel Castle in Cornwall was the real site of Arthur's Camelot.**

Arthur is supposed to have built a magnificent castle called Camelot for Queen Guinevere. It may have been at Tintagel Castle or Caerleon in Wales. Only their ruins survive today. Some historians now believe that Arthur was a real king, that he lived in the sixth century, hundreds of years before the age of knights and chivalry.

MAKING A ROUND TABLE

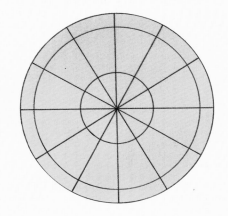

1. Using a compass, draw three circles. With a protractor and ruler, divide the circles into 12 segments each measuring 30 degrees.

2. Write your name and those of your friends around the edge. Draw a picture in each segment that says something about the person who will sit facing it. Color in the gaps.

TALES OF CHIVALRY

The minstrel ends the evening with a different legend: "An evil dragon rules the land. Many knights have tried to defeat him, but their bones now litter the fields. The dragon scorches the peasants' crops. In their terror, they have chained up a maiden as a sacrifice to the beast. A knight, St. George, gallops past her, and levels his lance at the fire-breathing dragon ..."

St. George was a third-century Christian from the Middle East who was beheaded for his beliefs. He became the patron saint of knights. Real knights also became saints. King Louis IX of France led expeditions to the Holy Land and died on crusade in 1270. He was made a saint after his death.

△ This fifteenth-century painting shows St. George as the ideal knight, risking his life to save the lady.

After hearing legends of chivalry, many knights joined special orders or brotherhoods. The Dukes of Burgundy founded a brotherhood called the Order of the Golden Fleece. Its members gave much of their money away to charity and held fantastic tournaments in the cities of Bruges and Ghent.

△ This precious badge of honor was worn by a herald of the Knights of the Golden Fleece.

DRAGON-SLAYERS

German legends tell of a dragon-slaying hero called Siegfried. He kills the dragon Fafner to save the world from an evil curse:

"Alone but trusting to his magic sword Nothung, Siegfried slashed the head of Fafner, burning his fingers in the serpent's red-hot blood."

△ This carving shows Sigurd killing a dragon.

Tales of chivalry were told all over Europe. St. George in England, Sigurd in Scandinavia, and Siegfried in Germany were all heroes who killed dragons. Another popular hero was Parsifal. He had to prove that his heart was pure before he could complete his quest. Such stories set a good example of chivalry to real knights.

KNIGHTS OF THE EAST

THE PERSIAN AND MONGOLIAN armies watch as two champions ride out from their ranks. Their ponies fly across the yellow desert sand. Each warrior fires an arrow but misses his target. They draw their long curved swords and clash in a fight to the death. No mercy is asked or given.

Asian warriors did not wear as much armor as European knights, but they were skilled horsemen. Their favorite weapons were the short bow and the curved *shamshir*, or saber. Some also used the *chakram*, a small steel hoop with a razor-sharp edge. They spun this on their fingertips and tossed it at the enemy.

△ A drawing of a duel between two legendary Persian warriors, Sohrab and Rustum

BUSHIDO

The Samurai knights of medieval Japan had a code similar to chivalry, called Bushido. Samurai were given these rules:

*"**Do honor to your family, Do honor to the Emperor, Do honor to your sword, Do honor to yourself.**"*

The Samurai were important warriors in Japan from the twelfth century onward. They lived a life of strict honor and spent much of their time training for war. In 1274, they saved Japan from the invasion of Kublai Khan's Mongol Horde.

△ This Samurai war fan had sharpened edges and was used as a weapon.

Samurai armor consisted of a metal breastplate and skirts that protected most of the body. Under this, the warrior wore long-sleeved vests made of leather and chain mail. Samurai armor had to be strong. Their swords, or *wakizashi*, were probably the sharpest ever made.

◁ Over their armor, the Samurai wore decorative beading and a fierce war mask, or *menpo*, to frighten their enemies.

39

THE LAST KNIGHTS

FINAL BATTLES

"**P**OISE YOUR MUSKET!" The soldier raises the wooden stock of his weapon and takes aim. An officer shouts the command: "Give Fire!" He lowers a smoldering match onto his musket's pan of gunpowder. A hot musket ball bursts out. The gun makes so much smoke that he cannot tell if he has hit or missed his target.

▷ Soldiers called *landsknechts* wore brilliant costumes instead of armor and carried guns instead of swords.

In 1494, the finest knights in Italy gathered under their lord's banner near the village of Fornovo. They expected to crush with ease a tiny French Army facing them across a stream. The knights charged, but were mowed down by musket balls. Armed with guns, even low-born peasants could defeat a noble knight.

ORDER OF THE GARTER

Some orders of chivalry survived the coming of guns. This knight wears the colors of the Order of the Garter, which was founded in 1348 as a feasting club for the English king's bravest knights. Its members still meet today at Windsor Castle on St. George's Day, April 23. They are no longer fighting knights, but are advisers of the British monarch.

After 1450, guns were a common sight on European battlefields. Many armies hired Swiss or German *landsknechts*. These were professional soldiers, cheap and easy to train. Their pikes could impale the mounted knight, and their musket shot could pierce his metal shell. The age of the expensive, mounted knight was coming to an end.

◁ Swiss mercenaries with muskets and pikes set an ambush for their opponents.

THE END OF CHIVALRY

The proud South American warriors bow down before the strange gods from the sea. The gods have six legs and two heads, one of a horse and one of a man. They have bright, shining skin, which cannot be pierced, and fire-shooting sticks that kill from far away. The warriors bow down before their conquerors.

After 1500, many knights from Spain and Portugal sailed to the newly discovered continents of North and South America in search of wealth and adventure. One of them, Hernando Cortés, conquered the lands of the Aztec people of South America with only 600 soldiers. Knights like Cortés were interested in gold, land, slaves, and power. The age of chivalry was over forever.

△ **Cortés and his army enter the Aztec capital of Tenochtitlán.**

Cannons flattened the knight's castle. Muskets peppered his armor. Chivalry was forgotten. In 1500, a soldier wrote: "In olden days, the greatest king was he who led the bravest and most virtuous knights. In these modern times, battles and wars are won by the king who has the largest treasury. Men now fight for their wages in gold, not for honor."

▽ Knights left behind castles like Karlstein, in the Czech Republic. Karlstein was said to contain a piece of the True Cross, which had been the quest of so many knights.

TIME LINE

600	800	1041	1066
Possibly the age when King Arthur ruled from Tintagel Castle.	Charlemagne's mounted knights defend his empire from the Vikings.	The Truce of God forbids knights to fight on three days of the week.	England is conquered by Norman knights fighting under Duke William.

1222	1243	1274	1346
St. George, the knightly saint, is given his own feast day of April 23.	The Grand Tournament is held to celebrate a five-year truce between France and England.	Samurai warriors help to save Japan from invasion by the Mongolian Horde.	Blind King John of Bohemia dies fighting in the Battle of Crecy.

1415	1439		1483
French knights are defeated by English and Welsh bowmen at the Battle of Agincourt.	The new army of Louis XI of France contains mercenary soldiers rather than the old-style knights of chivalry.		The College of Heralds is established by Edward IV of England to "preserve the study of chivalry."

1096	**1099**	**1100**	**1119**
Pope Urban II calls on the knights of Europe to crusade in the Holy Land.	Crusading knights capture Jerusalem and set up their own castle estates.	Wooden motte and bailey castles are replaced by castles with stone keeps.	Sir Hugh de Payns founds the Holy Order of the Knights Templar.

1348		**1370**	**1400**
Edward III founds the chivalrous Order of the Garter. Karlstein Castle, in the Czech Republic, is built.		Armor-piercing crossbows are first used in battle in Italy.	Coca Castle is built in Spain.

1494	**1500**	**1519**	
Italian knights are defeated by French cannons at the Battle of Fornovo.	Knights from Spain and Portugal sail in search of gold to the Americas.	Hernando Cortés conquers the Aztec empire with a small band of knights.	

GLOSSARY

Aztecs People of ancient Mexico.

caparison The colorful cloth used to decorate a warhorse.

chain mail Armor made from small iron rings linked together.

charger A knight's horse.

chivalry The laws of good behavior that knights were expected to follow.

coat of arms The design in heraldry used by a knight as his badge and worn on his costume, shield, and horse.

doublet A short, tight-fitting jacket.

emir A ruler of a Muslim city or country in the Middle Ages.

Frank A person of Western origin in the Middle East (especially a knight from Germany).

heraldry A system in which a knight could be recognized by his badge and colors.

jousting A sport in which two mounted knights charged each other with lances.

liege The lord to whom a knight owed loyalty and service.

marshal The castle official who was in charge of the stables.

medieval Of the Middle Ages, the period of European history lasting from about A.D. 1000 to 1453.

mêlée A brawl in the middle of battle, or a mock battle in tournaments where knights fought on foot.

minstrels Musicians or singers, who often recited poems.

Mongol Someone from Mongolia, Asia.

Muslims The Islamic peoples of Spain, North Africa, and the Middle East.

page A young boy sent to a castle to train as a knight.

pike A weapon with a long shaft and a blade with a spear-point and ax-head.

quest A knight's search, or the object of that search.

quintain A target for practicing the joust, often with a revolving arm holding a sandbag, which swung around to strike an unwary jouster.

serfs Peasants who worked and served on a knight's lands.

shrines Holy places often containing the bones or relics of a saint.

squire A knight's attendant, who was training to be a knight.

standard A flag with a distinctive design.

tabard A knight's or herald's short coat, showing a coat of arms.

tournament A meeting of knights for jousting and other games of combat.

truce A period in which fighting or violence was forbidden.

tunic A loose robe worn over armor.

virtuous Possessing moral qualities.

FURTHER INFORMATION

BOOKS & CD ROMS

BOOKS

Day, Malcolm. *The World of Castles and Forts*. New York: Peter Bedrick Books, 1996.

Gravett, Christopher. *Castle* (Eyewitness Books). New York: Knopf Books for Young Readers, 1994.

Macaulay, David. *Castle*. Boston: Houghton Mifflin, 1977.

MacDonald, Fiona. *A Medieval Castle* (Inside Story). New York: Peter Bedrick Books, 1993.

———. *A Samurai Castle* (Inside Story). New York: Peter Bedrick Books, 1995.

Platt, Richard. *Stephen Biesty's Cross-Sections Castle*. New York: Dorling Kindersley, 1994.

Steele, Philip. *I Wonder Why Castles Had Moats and Other Questions About Long Ago* (I Wonder Why). New York: Kingfisher Books, 1994.

Williams, Brian. *Forts and Castles* (See Through History). New York: Viking Children's Books, 1995.

World Book Staff. *Age of Knights and Castles* (Look At). Chicago: World Book, 1996.

CD ROMS

Castle Explorer (Dorling Kindersley)
The Herbalist (Multimedia CD-ROM)

INDEX

Numbers in **bold** refer to pictures and captions.

castles
    Alnwick **23**
    Chepstow 6, **6**
    Coca **18**
    Karlstein **43**
    Muiderslot 9, **9**
    Tintagel 35, **35**
    Windsor 41
Charlemagne 5
chivalry 6, 7, 9, 12, 17, 19, 22, 23, 31, 32, 35, 36, 37, 39, 41, 42, **43**
Christianity 5, 9, 15, 16, 17, 18, 19, 20, 23, 31, 36, 37, 43
crusades 16, **16**, 17, **17**, 18, 19, 20, 21, 28, 36

firearms 40, **40**, 41, 42, 43
food and drink 5, 7, 7, 8, **8**, 20, 24, 34
France 4, **8**, **12**, 16, 17, 28, 32, 37, 40
Franks 18, 20, 21, **20–21**, 28

George, St. 36, **36**
Germany **12**, 16, 27, 37, 41

heraldry 12, **12**, 13, **13**, 15, **26–27**, **28**, 31, 31, 32, 37

Holy Land 16, 17, 18, 19, 36
horses 4, 5, 7, **7**, 10, 11, 13, 19, 22, 23, 24, 28, **28**, 29, **29**, 30, 38

Italy 16, **16**, **17**, 40

Jerusalem 16, 18, 19
jousting 10, 14, **14**, 31, 32, 33, **32–33**

kings
    Arthur 34, **34**, 35
    Frederick II
      of Germany 21
    John (the Blind)
      of Bohemia 22
    Louis IX (Saint)
      of France 36
    Philip II of France 32
    Richard I (the Lionheart)
      of England 21
    Richard III
      of England 29

legends 34, 35, 36
Luttrell, Sir Geoffrey 7, **7**

mêlée 30, **30**
music 8, 20, 34, 36, 37
Muslims 16, 18, 19, 20, 21, **20–21**

Normans 4, **4–5**

orders 37
    Garter 41, **41**
    Golden Fleece 37, **37**
    Star 8, **8**

pages 8, **8**, 10
peasants 6, 11, **11**, 17, 30, 40

Saladin 19, 21
Samurai 39, **39**
Scotland 23, 25
ships 4, **4–5**, 16, **16**
Spain 18, **18**, 30, 42
squires 8, 9, **9**, 10, **10–11**, 12, **14**, 15, **24**, 26, **26–27**, 29

Templars 19, **19**
tournaments 30, **30**, 31, **31**, 37
training 8, 9, 10, **10–11**

vows 6, 7, 9, 15, 19

weapons and armor 4, 5, 9, 10, 12, 15, 22, 23, 24, 25, **25**, 26, 27, **26–27**, 28, 29, **29**, 31, **31**, 32, 33, 37, 38, 39, **39**, 40, 41

© Copyright 1998 Wayland (Publishers) Ltd.